If
you take
a careful look,
you'll see
how
creatures
in this book
are
CAMOUFLAGED
and out
of view—
although
they're right
in front
of you.

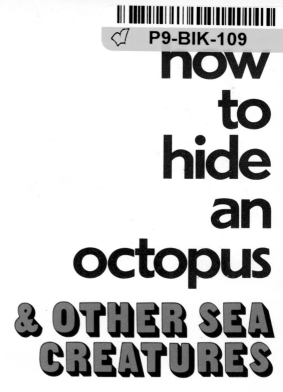

how
to
hide
an
octopus
& OTHER SEA CREATURES

BY RUTH HELLER

P9-BIK-109

 Kingfisher Books

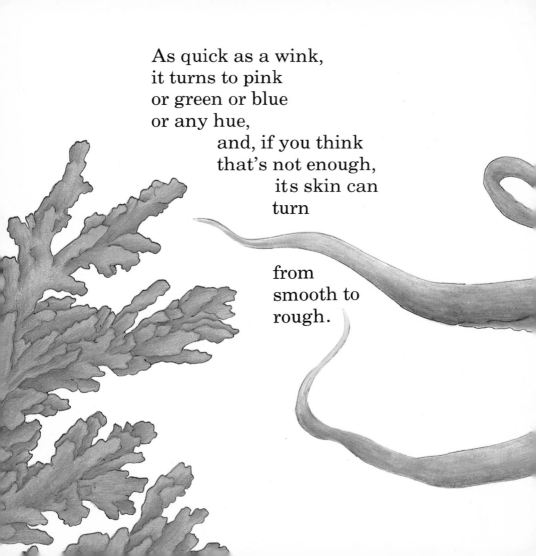

As quick as a wink,
it turns to pink
or green or blue
or any hue,
and, if you think
that's not enough,
its skin can
turn

from
smooth to
rough.

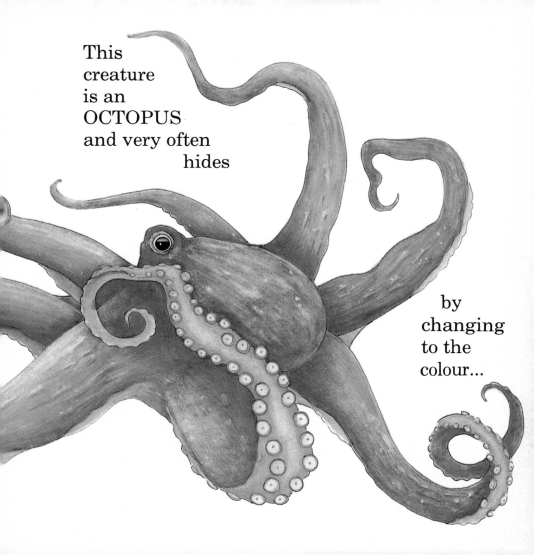

This
creature
is an
OCTOPUS
and very often
hides

by
changing
to the
colour...

over
which
it glides.

Its relative,
the
CUTTLEFISH,
could do the same
if he should wish.
The stripes that he is
sporting
show
that he's
been courting,
but
he can
make them
fade away...

slowly
or
without
delay.

The
SARGASSUM FISH,
grotesque
at
best,
looks
just
like…

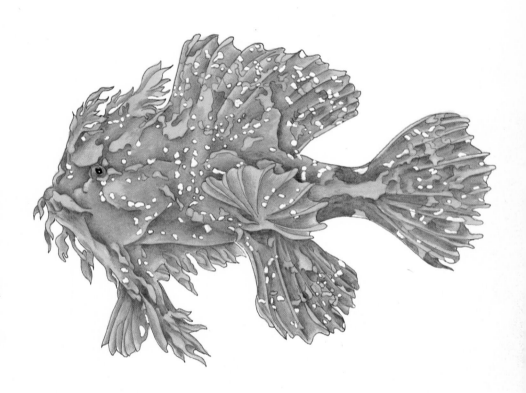

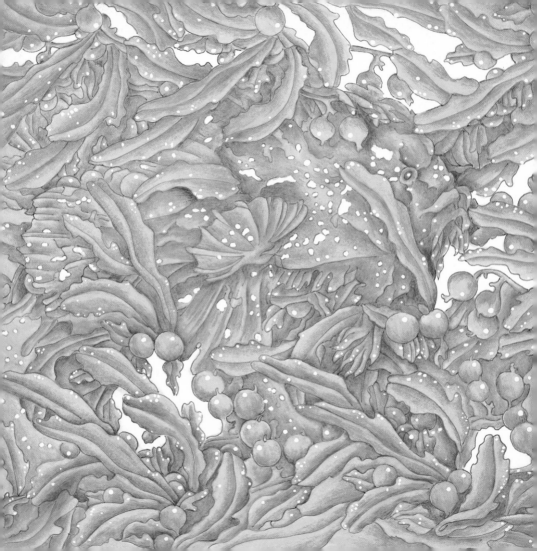

its
seaweed
nest.

The
  giant red
SEA DRAGON
    is

the most bizarre
of all the
creatures
seen so far,
with
ribbons of skin
that grow
from its chin
and
from its
belly and back.
They
spread
from its head
and trail from its tail,
and it's
easy to see
why its enemies fail
to find
where it feeds…

among
the
red
weeds.

The
SHRIMPFISH
hides
and
lives
and
dines
head
down
among
the
urchins'
spines.

Heads
up,
the
PIPEFISH
like
to
play
and
with
the
grasses
drift
and
sway.

The
BUTTERFLY
FISH

has been
designed
to
make
it
very
hard…

to
find.

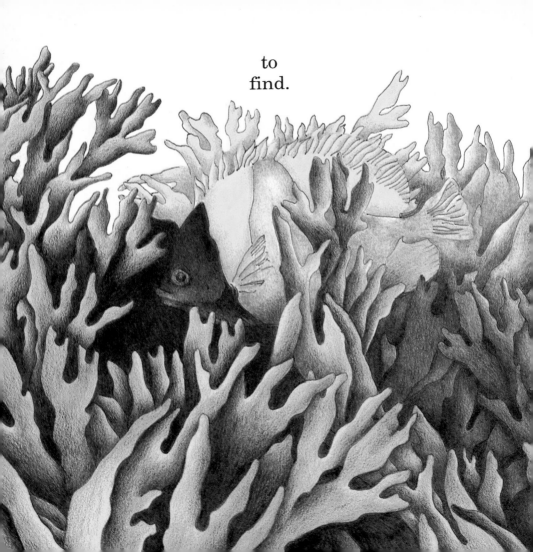

The
DECORATOR CRAB
is drab
and
will not rest
until it's dressed,

so
it proceeds
to don
some
weeds
and barnacles
and sponge,
you
see,

and
even
an...

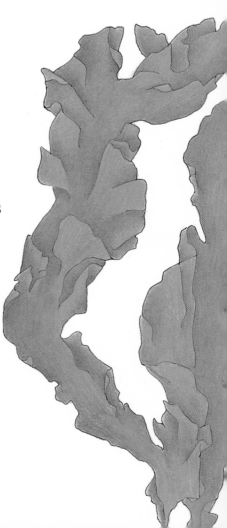

anemone.